D0696830

FAIRY TAIL

17

Hiro Mashima

WITHDRAWN
No longer the property of the
Boston Public Library.
Sale of this material benefits the Library.

Translated and adapted by William Flanagan
Lettered by AndWorld Design

Contents

Fairy Tail volume 17 1
Afterword 187
Explanations 189
Fan Art 191
Translation Notes 192
Preview 193

HIRO MASHIMA

Chapter 135: Priestess of the Sky 3

Chapter 136: Coffin 23

Chapter 137: The Girl and the Ghosts 43

Chapter 138: Didn't Count On 64

Chapter 139: Dead Grand Prix 83

Chapter 140: Slow Speed World 103

Chapter 141: Light 124

Chapter 142: Darkness 147

Chapter 143: Celestial Spirit Brawl 167

Published in serial form by Weekly Shônen Magazine 2009 Volumes 25 - 33.

Chapter 127, Priestess of the Sky

Remarks

In his youth he learned Ice Make Magic with Gray under the tutelage of Ur. He entered the guild Lamia Scale after losing to Gray in a battle to determine the fate of Ur's mortal enemy, Deliora. While Gray uses his Ice Make to create inanimate objects like weapons, Lyon's specialty lies in making ice creatures. Although he used to ignore Ur's teaching and practice one-handed Ice Make he later returned to two-handed Ice Make and progressed rapidly. He's risen to the level of guild ace and now takes high-level jobs.

Wendy ?
.....
Eh?
Eh?
!!!
SHUUU
RAIN

!
It's the Priestess of the Sky!
I'm sure of it...
What's wrong with Brain?
How should I know?
It means I've found something good!
What's that supposed to mean?!
...the Sky?
The Priestes of...
Kyaa!
Come!
!!

Wendy !!!!
Carla !!!
Eee!
FWURLURL
All's fair...
What do you think you're doing ...?!
... in money and war !!!!
DOOOM
KYAA!
KWAA!
GAH!
UWAA!

Ah!
GRABB
Huh?
!!!
CARLAA!!!
WENDY!!!
Wendy!!!!
Happy!!!!
NATSU! WAAAA!!!
GYULUM
KYAAAAAA!
DM
DM
DM
DM
We have no more use for you!
Vanish!!!

ドドド

!!!
DMP
GOMA
NYOOK
NYOOK
WHOOSH
IRON-ROCK WALL !!!!
GACH
GAM
GAM
GAM
GAM

DOGOGOON
Where are they ?!!
That was amazing!
You saved us. Thank you.
And a no-hidden-meaning "thank you" to you too.
Oooh! So smooth and shiny!
Jura-sama !!!

Dammit!!! They ran away!!!
They're gone!!!
I'm glad to see you're all right, Jura-san.
They were too strong for us.
We were pretty roundly beaten.
Wendy..
That wound...
It was a dangerous spot.
SHHP
じゃ
No.

The Oración Seis fled just as we were arriving. They must have been scared!
I was able to fight through it using Ichiya-dono's temporary "Pain Relieving Perfume."
You're falling apart!
My pain... is gradually fading away...
It smells nice!
Everyone partake of my Pain Relieving Perfume!
They took... Wendy and Happy...
They changed their name for him again...
That's our sensei for you!

G'NIM
NGAH!
Natsu !!!
ZHOOM
BUT WHERE ?!!!
FLAFF
FLAFF
DOWHUMP
What did you say?!!
You're just like Happy.
It's only natural that you wouldn't know it...
This is a magic called Aera.
FLAFF
FLAFF
A cat is flying around.
Wings?!

While the situation with Wendy and the male cat is upsetting...
...I think we all realize that this enemy is not one we should face without a plan.
ROLL
!!
TWIRL
Also...
The enemy is more powerful than we predicted.
It is as Carla-dono says.
Urn...
Urg...
Erza! Hang in there!!!
My Pain Relieving Perfume does not work on her...? Inconceiv-able!!!

!!!
Kyaaa!
SLUMP

Eh?
Lucy... Forgive me... I need your belt...
ZLMM
する
GACHIK

Erza!!!

I can't fight as I am now.

GRNN
ギリ
GRNN
ギリ
GRNN
ギュッ
Wh-What are you doing...?

KACHANG

DOOM
Cut it off!
HAHH
HAHH
HAHH
What kind of idiocy are you spouting?!
!!!
!!!
Do it!
Lyon, you... !!!
GRATCH
Understood. I'll do it.

But...
mmm
We cannot allow this woman to die here and now!
Don't !!!
Don't do it, Lyon!!!
Do it!!!! Now!!!!
What would *you* know about reality?!
Just how divorced from reality are you Fairies?!
HYUU
It is Erza-dono's wish!
You don't have to do it!
Will you stop this ?!!!

GACHIKK
I'm saying there may be another way, so don't take the first simple-minded solution that comes to you!
You cretin! Are you saying that her arm is more important than her life?
WHUDD
Erza!!!
This is bad!! If we don't do something, the poison in her body...
Ah...

Wendy could save her.

We should combine strengths and save Wendy!
And maybe that male cat along the way.
This is no time for squabbling among allies.

Healing Magic...? isn't that one of the lost magics?
Does that have anything to do with this "Priestess of the Sky" thing?

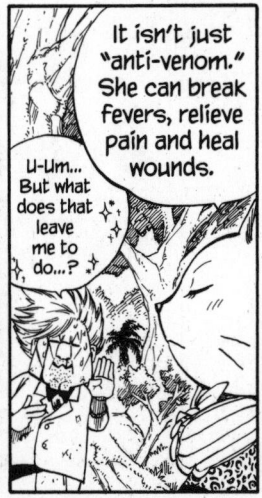
It isn't just "anti-venom." She can break fevers, relieve pain and heal wounds.
U-um... But what does that leave me to do...?

So that girl has some anti-venom magic?
That's amaz-ing!

Dragon Slayer?!
We'll save the details for later. Still, there isn't much more you need to know.
She is a Sky Drago Slayer.
Sky Dragon Wendy.

Right now, we need Wendy.
They need Wendy too, but I don't know why.
...That means...
There is one thing to do.
We must rescue Wendy-san.
For Erza's sake.
And Happy's!
Right !!!!

Let's go !!!!!
Yes !!!!!

Chapter 136, Coffin

Remarks

She holds a grudge against the demon Deliora, who murdered both her parents when she was very young. She left Lamia Scale to follow Lyon in an attempt to take down Deloria, rejoining later to take on jobs in earnest. Her magic is Doll Attack Magic, with which she can manipulate anything non-human: trees, rocks, even Celestial Spirits. She claims that when she turned seventeen, she gave herself something of an attitude makeover.

SSSH
SSSH
SSSH
SSSH
SSSH
SSSH
SSSH
SSSH
This was the capital of an ancient civilization.
HYOOOOOO
These caves were where the village worshipped their gods.
They say a priestess would enter here to receive the words of the gods.

Don't get violent!!! She's a girl, okay?!!
WHAMM
Kyaaa!
Kyaaa!
Happy!!!
Flurg!
MFrr!
MRFLL
GYUU
KYUUUU
POIT
Humph.

I get it! You'll sell her for money!
Doesn't look like it to me.
Does she have something to do with Nirvana?
Brain, what's with the girl?
She's adept at the healing arts of Sky Magic.
TSK
This little girl...
I certainly smell money now!
ZZZ
ZZZ
The lost magic?
Healing Magic?

Exactly!
We'll resurrect *him!*
WHOOSH
!!!
You can't mean ...?!!
Yes you will.
I guarantee it.
I-I'm...not going to do anything to help bad people like you!!!
You certainly will...
...revive him.
URRRR...

That makes sense... With him, we will have pretty much found Nirvana.
Even at my fastest, it'll take an hour.
Racer, bring him here.
Whatever it takes.
Balam Alliance
But we won't need to if that guy is revived.
Cobra, Hoteye, Angel...
There is always that one-in-a-million chance. Midnight and I will remain here.
I don't think Mid s interest- ed in going anywhere ...
...go out and continue your search for Nirvana.
What... kind of magic is that...?
This Nirvana ...?
...gets a million jewels!!! I'm in!!!
Hey, you want to make a competi- tion of it? The first to find it...
Okay, I guess we're heading out.
Way too much.

It takes darkness and light...
...and reverses them.

You aren't going yourself?
All active parties have entered the forest.
Please, everybody... Hurry!
PUUN!
Such humility...
PEEP
PEEP
PEEP
How can I just leave Erza?
And no matter how you look at it, I have the least battle strength of anybody.
Each story, way too over-blown.
You put the Master of Phantom out of action...
I've heard rumors about you. They say you defeated a three-meter tall gorilla...
And you defeated a thousand-man army alone in Akarifa.
PEEP
PEEP
PEEP
PEEP
PEEP

You're nicer than I figured.
How can any man just leave two women alone?
PEEP
PEEP
PEEP
PEEP
PEEP
You asked me, but why aren't *you* going?

Even if we can free Wendy and Happy...
...it'll mean nothing if they don't know where we are.
PEEP
PEEP
PEEP
PEEP
PEEP
Besides, my magic will let everyone know where we are.

They said she's a Sky Dragon Slayer!

So what does she eat?
Is that any different from breathing?
Who knows?
Does it taste good?
Air.
Me?
I had her apply to this mission thinking she might meet you.
You're both dragon slayers, right?

I thought perhaps you may know where it went.
SHK
SHK
...vanished seven years ago.
She says that the dragon who taught her dragon slayer magic...
SHK
SHK
...and Wendy's dragon, all seven years ago...
Igneel, Gajeel's dragon...
TMP
TMP
Who knows?
Hey! Did it disappear on July 7th?
I think it was called the "Sky Dragon Grandine," maybe.
TMP
TMP
TMP
TMP
Wh-What's this?!!
The old man said it, right? That wasn't Dragon Slayer magic.
Oh, yeah! What about Laxus?!
KRAKK
NGAAH!
SKRRCH

The trees...
They're black...
Th-This is creepy...
Who ?!!
Waahoo! It's such a powerful magic that the Earth itself is dying, Big Brother Gatô!
SHK
!!
They say it's from the influence of Nirvana, Big Brother Zatô.
SHK

W-Wait a moment...
RUSTLE
RUSTLE
RUSTLE
GM
GM
GM
GM
GM
Did I, Big Brother Zatô?
You already said that, Big Brother Gatô.
They it's the ence of ana...
ISA
SA
We're sur-rounded !!!!

Hey!! Another monkey has joined them!
Just remembering... what that woman did...
Th-These guys are Fairy Tail!!! It's all their fault...
Wow! Monkeys! There are two monkeys over there!
Waahoo! Let's play for a while!
We're *Naked Mummy,* working under Oración Seis!
SALSA
くるくる
TWIRL TWIRL
Oo! Ook! Perfect timing! Ook!
Perfect timing!
What are you guys talking about?!
So the enemy... weren't just six wizards...?! We fell into a trap...

We're going to make you spill where this secret base is.
We're coming for you, Happy!! Wendy!!
ZLOOM
ZLOOM
KRIKK
Those stupid brats are dissing us!
We're *Naked Mummy*, working under Oración Seis!
You idiots are gonna die!
Don't they even know what danger they're in?!
What's with these Fairy Tail wizards ...?!

What are they doing in a place like this...?!
Black Unicorn ?!!
You're saying we're surrounded?!
What is this exactly ...?
CROWD
CROWD
You mean they had troops waiting in ambush?
I-I mean, I'm not anybody you should attack... Meeeen!
Wait ...
I-I'm just a lost man...who got...separated from his group...

This thing's heavy ...
Eee!
A coffin ?!!
No one is faster than you.
I couldn't get any speed carrying it!
ZUCHUNK
You will cure him.
KREEEE
You must cure him!
PACHINK
Right! Never!
M-Me...? No, I would never do something like that!!!
GACHINK
CHANK
I dis-agree.
GANK GANK GANK
CHRM CHRM CHRM CHRM CHRM
PACHINK
Wendy, you will cure this man.

!!!
DOOOM

In other words, he is a man who knows where Nirvana is.
This man is named Jellal!
At one time he even infiltrated the Magic Council.
He was bathed in Ethernanos and became this way.
You know him?!
Jellal...
Eh?!
Eh?
Jellal...?
You're the only one who can bring him back.
You owe him... your life, right?

FAIRY TAIL

フェアリーテイル

LAMIA SCALE

Name: Jura Neekis **Age:** 27

Magic: Master of All Earth Magics

Likes: His guild **Dislikes:** Green peas

WIZARD GUILD 33

Remarks

Jura is considered the ace of the Lamia Scale guild and one of the Ten Wizard Saints, the ten best wizards on the continent. He is extremely powerful in Earth-type Magics–because he can take the softest sand and change it into iron-hard rock, he has been given the name Iron Rock Jura. He loves his guild and looks after its members, including Lyon and Sherry. Once while snacking on green peas as a child, he accidentally popped a green caterpillar into his mouth and can no longer stomach green peas.

Chapter 137, The Girl and the Ghost

Whoooaa!!!!
RAHH!!!!!
Gwaah!
GAHH!
GYEEH!
DOGOOOM
!
WHAKK

DWIRRL
Eee!
PACHIK
PACHIK
PACHIK
PACHIK
Gwaah!
Gyaa!
Ugaah!
ZUCHAKAKAKAK
ZUGANN
Eat hot lead from my magic shot gun!!!
DAK DAK DAK DAK DAK
GACHANK
Those little...

HE'S A MONSTER!
SHUU
SHUU
SHUU
SHUU
SHUU
Heey !!!!
Ha haaa !!!!
Let's get into it too, Big Brother Zatô.
ZHUU
It looks like they aren't such bad fighters, Big Brother Gatô.
GWOOO
DOKAM
VWAA

He used the council to fire Etherion down on us!
Know him?! He was the guy who tried to murder Erza!
You know him, Happy?
Jellal... You mean *that* Jellal?
No!!! You mustn't, for any reason, bring that guy back !!!
But... to you, he's your savior.
That guy's a ghost who was possessed by a ghost. An insane idealist.
So he's still alive...
I guess that was true, huh...?

MLIGM GM
GM GM GM
Hurry up! Revive him!
Wendy !!!
ZATCH
!!!

BONK
OWW!
DOKAM
GISSH
No, don't !!!!
Revive him!
It should be easy for you!
PLIP
PLIP
But even so...
...he saved my life...
Jellal is a bad man!!! And he'll just take Nirvana for himself anyway!

I loved him...
ボロ
PLIP
ボロ
PLIP
PLIP
ZZZ
ZZZ
ZZZ
Jellal would never do anything like that!!!
Somebody must have been manipulating him! I'm sure of it!!!
What are you saying?! We were right there on the scene...
I heard...that he did some bad things, but I don't believe it...

Fine.

Wendy !!!
Please!! Give me some time t think about it!!!

Five minutes.

Natsu ...
This is bad. Come quick, okay?

BUH HAHH ...
DAH HAHH ...
PANT
WHEEZE
PANT
WHEEZE
PANT
WHEEZE
SALSA

They fought better than I expected...
What was with those guys? I thought they were supposed to be small fry.
SLUMP
GWEEH
What were you two thinking?!!!
What did you expect?!! You fought an entire guild!!!
GANCH
You think I'd tell you, fool! Waa ha ha...
GWIP
GWAAH...
Hey! Hey, Mr. Waahoo Monkey!!!!! Where's this base of yours?!!!

You guys are just too violent!
Hey!!! Big monkey!!!
Where is your stronghold?
A village of the ancients?
An abandoned village to the west?

What about you, Jura?
Lyon and Sherry, head west.

...they've given us a clue to their base.
They dug their own graves. By sending those people to eliminate us...

The Oración Seis?!
There's a huge amount of magic energ heading this way.
I will wait for it here.

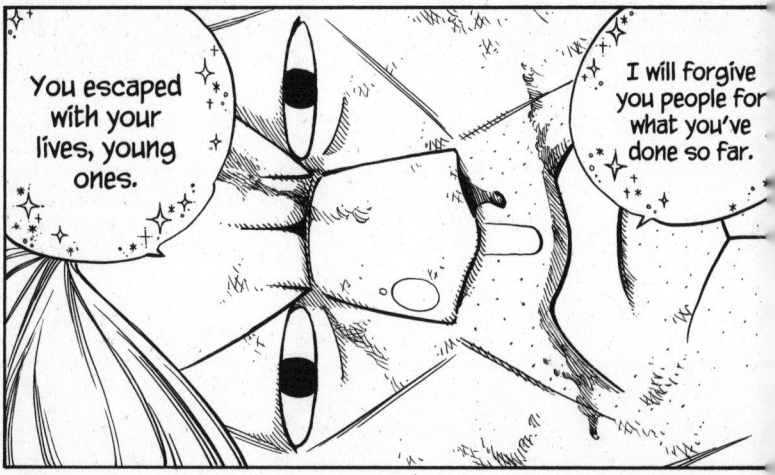
You escaped with your lives, young ones.
I will forgive you people for what you've done so far.

So please, spare me!!!!
I... I'm only twenty-nine years old !!!
Shaddap!
You know, you're an annoying old guy!
Why don't one of you take me on in a one-on-one fair fight! That's what young people do, right?!
I know!! Let's do this!!! And I'll go all out too!
And they say that the smart hawk hides his claws...
Shut up, you pig!!!
Well, you realize that I don't go all out unless there's a pretty lady watching.
Okay, maybe I took you guys for lightweights a little...

Oh... You mean with that copy magic of hers?
I hear there was some info that Angel-sama forgot to gather.
Meeen!

Y-Young men!!! One must always obey the orders of one's superiors !!!
Let's just knock him off once and for all!
Why do we gotta capture that creep anyway?

Wendy!!!!
Happy!!!!
Hey! The enemy might be around here too, you know!

Here?

!!
It's
atsu!
Wendy!!
aaah!
Those
trash...
Okay.
Racer,
don't
let them
get any
closer.
G'YUUM

!!!
GWOOOO
ZUGYAN
Gwaah!
Gahaah!
It's him again!!
KAK
SHUSH
KAK

You think I'd let you do that?!
Got it!!!
Leave him to me! You hurry and get down there, Natsu!
Carla, now!!! Wings !!!
Gyaa !!
ZLUNCH
Ohh!!
ZLIPP
KEEEEN
If it's the only way, take this route!
You little ...
Eh? What ?!
Let's go!!!
PYOING
PACHIKCHIKCHIKCHIK
GYUOOO

KYAAA!!
SHAAAAA
HYOOOO!!!!
So you managed to stop me, huh?
You just slipped and fell. That's all.

Happy !!!!
Wendy !!!!
You got sick?!
Urp...
THUMP
TMP
Happy !!!
They're in there!
ZAAAATSUUU!!
Wh-What is this supposed to be...?!!
You're joking...!!!

You're joking ...!!!
Wh-What is this supposed to be... ?!!

Urn...
I'm sorry ...

Natsu

B-BMP
B-BMP

I'm sorry...
I just...

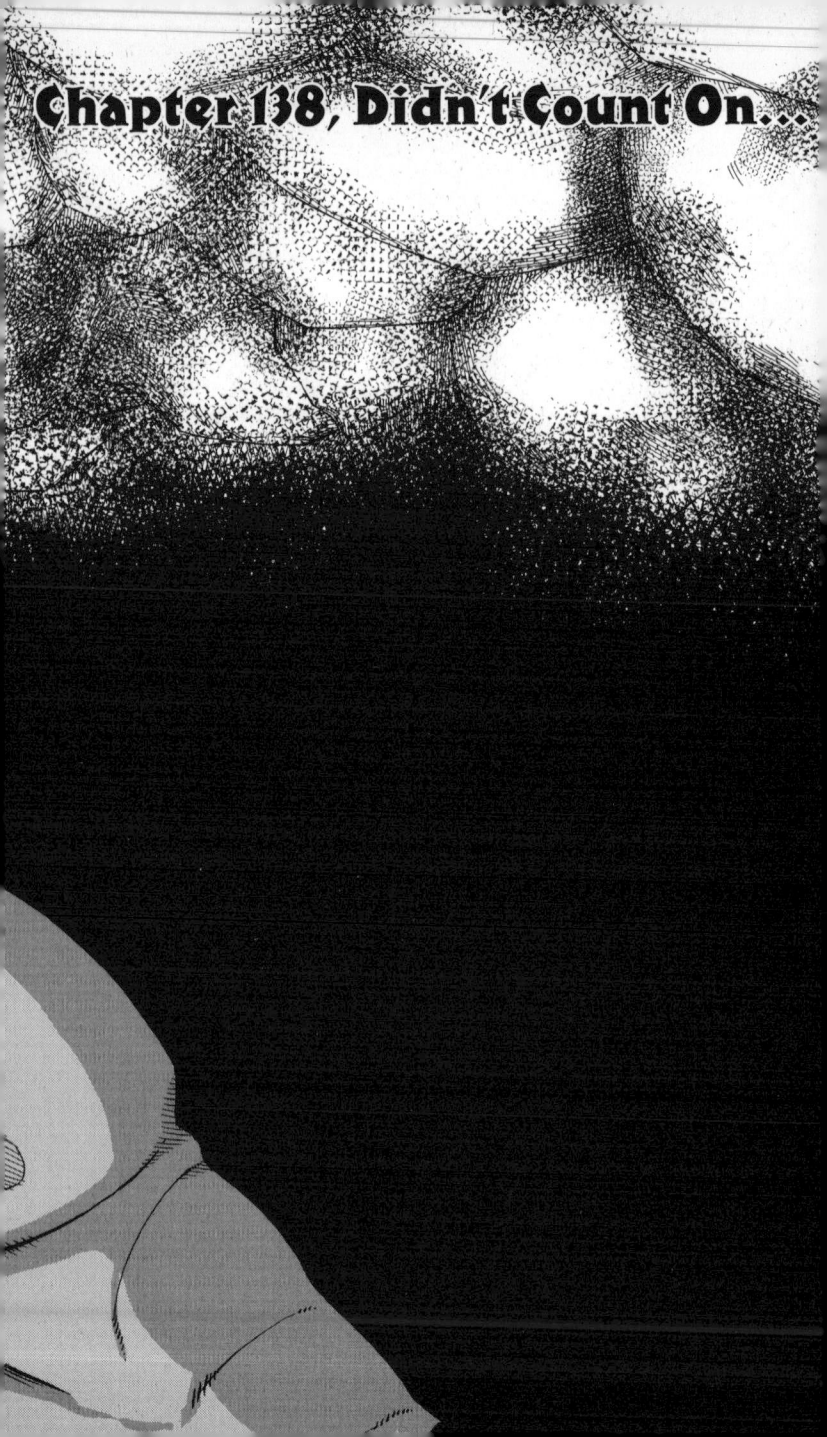

Chapter 138, Didn't Count On...

Jellal...
What do you ink you're doing?! sing that ower carelessly...
Wendy!! You used your curing magic ?!!
He... saved my life... so...
PLIP
PLIP
SNIFF...
SNIFF...
I'm...so sorry...
WHUD
Wendy!
SLUMP

Wh-What...are you doing here...?
DMM

GWOOM
Natsu !!!
UWAAAA!
ZUGAMGAMGAM
Jellal.
KRAKL
KRAKL
You always had an excess of power.
KRMBLE

WHOOSH
!
What ?!!!
KRMBL
KRMBL
KRMBL
KRMBL
GWAAAAH!

ZZZZ
ZZZZ
ぐー
ぐー
CHIK
つか
CHIK
つか
CHIK
つか
CHIK
つか
SST
すー
GWAMPH
わぶ
ばっ
Jellal !!!!
CHIK
つか
CHIK
つか
CHIK
つか
CHIK
つか
I have no idea what that person is, but the first order of business is to take Wendy back!
That bastard !!!!
He left.
Where is he ?!!

I know !!!!
You want Erza to live, don't you?!!!
Let's go!!!! Happy!!!!
Aye!!!!
Jellal...
KRMBL
KRMBL
.....
GYUUUUM

But...he should never have felt that kind of enmity for me...
KRMBL
KRMBL
I didn't count on that...
No... Removing his restraints was my mistake, perhaps...?
!
Should I have questioned him about our goal Nirvana when he was asleep?
You can't be trying to get Nirvana for yourself, can you?!!!
Jellal !!!!

I won't permi it!!!!
Nirvana belongs to us!!!! I won't let anyone else have it!!!!
Jellal has run off!!!!
Go after him!!!! Where he goes...
Cobra!!! Do you hear me?!!!
...is where Nirvana wi be!!!!

I can hear Jellal's footsteps too.
Okay!
Yeah, I heard you!
GAMM
KHH...
Tsk!
ZUDOON
WHOOSH
!!!

My code name is Racer.
THIP
How fast can that guy go ...?
Hey, Creep ...!
KAK
KAK
KAK
I'm faster than anyone. Faster than anything!
GWIP
SHAKEEN
Grimoire Heart
I just run.
ORACIÓN SEIS
RACER

GEEEEEEN
!!
Hm?
Impossible!!! Brain was in there! How could they possibly ...?!!
They got 'em out!!!
?!
Natsu!!! Dodge him !!!!
ZUBOSSH
KSSH
KSSH
Dammit!! You're not going anywhere!!!
DM
DM
DM
DM

BAKEEEN
WHOA!
WAA!
KYAAA
GRATCH
がしっ
SKRRRCH
HYUUUU
ZUDOOON
GAH
Oh, no !!!!
Carla !!!
Happy !!!

Ice Make ...
I said you're not going anywhere !!!
ZAASH
Dammit !!!
SLUM
DOGWOOM
GWUUH!
PACHIK
PACHIK
PACHIK
... RAMPART !!!!

ヒビキ
KRAKK
ヒビキ
KRAKK
ヒビキ
KRAKK
ガガガガ
GM
GM
GM
GM
パキ
KRAKL
パキ
KRAKL
パキ
KRAKL
ズズズズ
ZMM
ZMM
ZMM
ZMM
ZMM
But... you went and used up too much magic power!
Who cares?! Just go!
Go... I told you that I'd take care of him, right?
HAHH ハア
HAHH ハア
HAHH ハア
Gray.

I'll die before I let him ge beyond th point!!!!
Go!!!! Get to Erza !!!!
Of course she is!
Erza's going to live!!! You hear me ?!!!
ZHOOM
Hyooooo !!!!

Ice can even stop a person from aging.
I'll stop you a lot more than that.
That... makes the second time you've stopped me!
You can spend eternity and never pass us.
Your whole life, you'll be staring at a fairy's tail!

SHK
SHK
Erza...

Chapter 139, Dead Grand Prix

DMP
DMP
DMP
DMP
Jellal...
You big creep...
What were you doing in a place like this?!

Can you hear me?
That voice...

!
Natsu-kun!

It's me... Hibiki of the Blue Pegasus.
Thank goodness... I've been worried since I haven't been able to connect with anyone.
PEEP
PEEP
PEEP
PEEP

...so I'm going to speak directly to your mind.
It's possible that he can hear every word we say...
PEEP
PEEP
PEEP
PEEP
PEEP

STAY QUIET. ONE OF OUR ENEMIES HAS INCREDIBLY GOOD HEARING.
Where are you?!

I'm going to upload a map to your head. It will lead you to us.
Get here as quick as you can.

She's here.
EXCELLENT. THAT'S NATSU FOR YOU.

Ohh ?!!
What's this? What's this?!!
I know where Erza is now!!! But wait, I think I always knew it!
GET HERE FAST, NATSU-KUN!

JEEEEE

PING

It's a method of compressing information so it can be shared with others much faster than using speech.
PEEP
PEEP
My magic, Archive. It's information compression magic.
How'd you do that?
But I'm glad that Wendy's safe.
The very concept of using magic to turn information into data is, in itself, new.
I've never heard of that magic.
Hang in there!!
Just a little bit longer, Erza...

I'm going to protect you...

...at least until Natsu gets back.

I promise !!!

You managed to stop me twice ...

You're making it so I can't live up to my name.

If I felt like it, I could catch up to that kid, but...

SHUUM

...I won't be able to rest until I kill you!

I'll stop you again!!!
ORACION SEIS
Once I've done that, I'll have plenty of time for the chase.
!
SHUUM
When did he...?!!
Let the Dead Grand Prix...
WHOOSH
...BEGIN !!!!
VROOOOM
VROOOM
OOOOOM
OOOOOO
OOON
WOOSH
!!

Wha --?!
VROOOOO
VRMM
LWOON
LWOON
A huge number of Wizard Motor Bikes ...!!!
GAH!
GONCH
Whoa!
It's a motor show from hell.
VWOON
VWOON

GANCH
GAHAHH!
NOW DANCE !!!!
OOOON
Maybe ...
..I can ride one?
ACHIK
It even comes with an SEP plug!
SEP
!!
WHOOSH

Let's get this thing going !!!!
DM
DM
DM
DM
DM
DM
Just to warn you, there aren't any rules.
That's good! You really want to race me?!
GMM

ICE MAKE: LANCE !!!!
ZUGAKGAKGAKGAKGAK
PALUUU
VWAA
GRMM
GRMM
GRMM
!!
WHOA!
SKRRCH
SKRRCH
Tires ?!!

KAKK
GAGOOM
GAKON
GWOOOO
DM
DM
DM
DM
DM
DM
GYUOOOOOOOO

BATATATATATA
GAHH!
KACHIK
OOOOOOOO
This is for Erza...
VWOOO
I an't Ford lose !!!
What's wrong, pretty boy?
VWOOM
DM
DM
SKRRRCCH
Dam-mit!
OOOON

And one of the Oración Seis!!!
Gray ?!!
Lyon!!!
Just get on!!!
What was that?!
DM
DM
DM
You're in just the righ place!!
Get on!!!
Don't worry!! Natsu rescued her!!!
What about Wendy ?!
Lyon-sama!!!
What do you think you're doing?!
WHOOSH
DOGWOOOOOO

And 'll show you the asics of creation magic!
Then you should watch very closely!
'on't ve me hat!
Hmph!
VROOOOOOO
But I'm kind of hoping you can take this guy out for me.
DM
DM
DM
I can't use my magic very well while driving.
You...
.use both ands ow...?
"You're such a waste. You haven't changed. You still have to use both hands in your magic."
Ice Make...
THOK
!
ん
That's what our teacher taught us, right?

What ?!
EAGLE !!!!
ZUGAKGAKGAKGAK
KEEEEN
Playtime is over!
GYAAOO

DOGOOOM
HAMMER !!!!
DOOOM
KEEEN
BWOOON
Ice Make... Ape!!!!
KEEEN

BAKIK
ばっ
ばさ
BAKIK
You can follow his movement if you concentrate !!!
Concen-tration ...
Right !!!
ばさ
BAKIK
VWA
VWA
VWA
Calm down!!! Incoming at four o'clock !!!
Here we go, Lyon!!!
ばっ
WHOOSH
On my signal, fire with every-thing you got!!!!
I see him now !!!!
Now!!! Fifty meters in front of us!!!!
Why would Lyon-sama strip ...?
Why the strip ...?

SNOW DRAGON !!!!
ICE GEYSER !!!!
KEEEEEEN
GYUAAAA
FLAFF
He sped up even more!!!
Wha--?!!

KHH!
BAKIK
Over here
GACH
GAH!
SHAEEEEEN
He's good ...
Is that the Oración Seis?!
ZAASHH

You can attack as much as you like. It'll never hit me!
Nobody can match my speed!
I need your full attention, Gray.
Now... I think it's time to end this!
Then I'll go get that girl back.
I've found his weakness.

Remarks

A long-time top-ranker in the Weekly Sorcerer's poll of "Wizards You Wish Were Your Boyfriend." It's said that many female wizards, bewitched by his looks, try to join Blue Pegasus.

Archive magic lets information be compressed and sent to a recipient. He can also organize information and oversee battles. He has no steady girlfriend, but there are always rumors flying around who he's seeing. A legend states that he once dated 18 women at the same time (the truth is unconfirmed).

Chapter 140, Slow Speed World

WHISPER
ゴニョゴニョ
WHISPER
ゴニョゴニョ
WHISPER
ゴニョゴニョ

WHISPER
ゴニョゴニョ
WHISPER
ゴニョゴニョ
WHISPER
ゴニョゴニョ
WHISPER
ゴニョゴニョ
WHISPER

Hm?

...I don't need you anymore !!!
!!
PACHIK
PACHIK
PACHIK

What was that?!

And that's the reason why...

PACHIK
PACHIK
PACHIK
PACHIK
PACHIK
PACHIK CHIK
Lyon !!!!
You little ...
!
Lyon-sama !!!
Don't get the wrong idea.
A fight between allies?
He is *not* my ally.
We just happened to have the same teacher.
That was all.
Just stay there and watch.

But Lyon-sama...
I want no objections from you!!! This is a battle that Lamia Scale is taking control of!
Y-Yes, sir!!!
Aw, man!
It's that kind of vanity that can lead to a loss!!!!
DMM
Well... You guys never had a chance of winning in the first place!!!!
Wood Doll!!!!
WHOOSH
GRN
WHOOSH

GAMM
Ah!
You're too slow !!!!
GYULUN
Over here!!!
TMP
TMP
TMP
BAKOOM
OOOOOO
DMP
Slow, slow, slow !!!!
GYAOOOOO

No matter what speed you go at, you only have one attack.
Your weakness is you have no real attack strength.
シャキィン!
SHAKEEEN
Ice Make: Hedgehog !!!!
What ?!!
SKRRRCH
ズーン
ZHULIM
.....
What's the matter? Come at me with your famous speed!

!!!
DOGWOOM
You unde estimat me.
DOGWOOM
Do you think I show everything I've got when I'm up against a low-ranking opponent?
GWAHAH

Where do you think you're going?!!
DMP
SKRRRCH
ZUSSH
GWAAH!
GANCH
Hey, hey! Where's that overwhelming strength from when you started out?!
Lyon-sama...

KRAKON
GEEE!
GAH!
BAKAKK
Kh...
Aar...
KYUUM
KYUUM
H-
How fa
are you
plannin
to go
...?!
ZUGANDANGANGAM
GWAAAAH!!

!!!
SHING
GAHAAH!
ZUCCCH
GAN
With my speed, no matter what kind of magic you try, I can cut your throat first.
You said that I always use the same attack, huh?
But for attacks like this, my little blade is best.
I'm one of the Oración Seis!
Young kids always act puffed up, and that's okay. But this time you picked the wrong guy for that.

The six demons! The six prayers!!
The six pillars that will never crumble!
HA
HAH
HAHH
But when somebody tries to shake those pillars...
...they always die!
GWIIIIN
I... knew it...
?
When I saw a far-off bird flying incredibly fast...
...I thought I had figured out... your magic power.
?!
Your magic doesn't raise your speed at all.
It reduces your opponent's... Or I should say the speed of everything else within a certain area.

...can take away that speed!
In other words, you lowered my speed. That's all.
And as long as your magic only works in a limited area, anybody who sees you from outside that area...
DOOOM
PACHAAAAL

Wha...
PAKACHAAK
Th-That's why you ran as far away from him as you could...?!
I see. Now I can see it all.
But at that distance, he can't possibly hit me!!!
Yes, he can.
No matter what the try to do...
GRN
GRN
GRN
When Fairy Tail wizards put their hearts into it...
... they're the strongest in the world.

DWOOO
ZUDOOON
My prayer
...was to...!
...be the fastest ever...

GUAAAHHH!!!!!

I really thought you had turned on your ally.
"Did it"? With five of them left?
You did it, Lyon.
WOBBLE
Humph.
That's my elder disciple for you.
It isn't over yet !!!!
Don't try to make fun of me.
Can you stand?
GRN
GRN
GRN
WOBBLE

Dammit ...
LLUMP
ガシッ
You're kid-ding ...
Those are explosive lacrima ?!!!
In the name of the Oración Seis!!!!
I swear I'm not going down alone !!!!
ジャラ
SWIH
THONK
I'm taking one of you with me!!!!
hat kid'll be the leath of me...
Lyon-sama !!!!
Lyon !!!

DOGWOOMM

Lyon !!!!
ゴゴゴゴゴゴゴゴ!
GO GO GO GO GOOOOM
ズキィ!!…
ZHAAN
Arggh …
I made light of my enemy…
KLANK
RATTLE
Ohhh…
KANK
Does that mean one corner of the Six Demons has crumbled …?
FFT
Racer is…
SST
… dead …

I want them all dead!!! Every single one!!!!
BLINK
Mid-night !!!
I never expected to awaken him...
TREMBLE
Okay...
..Father.
ORACIÓN SEIS
MIDNIGHT

Chapter 141, Light

FAIRY TAIL
XXX

FAIRY TAIL

ooooooooo.

Th-That can't be...
Lyon-sama went...

Lyon.

Whose fault is this?

Why... would Lyon-sama...

Why...

He wouldn' die in that! We're goin to look for him!!!!
DMP
DMP
Come on !!!!

Come out!!
I know you're here.
Hyah !!!
WHSH
WHSH
That's one of the Ten Wizard Saints for you.
!!!
GWNYAAN
VCCCH
GYAAA
GWOON

My magic is to make the ground soft. And your magic is to harden it.
Now... Do we see which is better?
Of course there is no greater or lesser magic
VSSH
The one with the highest ideals always wins!
Oh, you're wrong. No matter the era, the ones who always win...
GRINN
...are always the rich!
ORACIÓN SEIS
HOTEYE

SHFF
ガサ
ガサ
SHFF
ナツばーーーっ
DAWHOOSH
I made it!!!!
Natsu !!!!

Calm down, Natsu!
Wake up, Wendy!!! Please, we need you to save Erza!!!!
GLUNK
GLUNK
SHAKA
SHAKA

Oh, yeah !!
Save that for later. First we need Wendy!
So what happened? I suddenly had this image of a map in my head...

I'm sorry... I...

!!!
Eee !!
ZUSH
ZUSH
ZUSH
ZUSH

Poison ?

Please save her!!! I'm begging!!!
GAMPH
We don't care about that right now!! Erza's been bitten by a poisonous snake!!!
.....

?!

Please... Save Erza !!!
We'll need Erza's power in our battle with the Oración Seis.
How long do you plan on staying there, you sluggard ?!
Thank goodness...
S-Sure, I will!!! Yeah!!! I'll do it!!!
I'll give it my best!
PIIING
They say Jellal did terrible things to Erza-san...
PAAAAA

He couldn't have...

SHK
SHK

He's stopped!

If I just heard his heart's voice, I wouldn't have to follow him!
He's a weird one. I can't hear his heart's voice.
STPP

What is this place...?!!
I didn't know that a place like this was in the forest!
PAKOO
Could it be that Brain nailed it?
That Nirvana is right here...

GOOOM
Ohh!!!
ZWAAAAA
Now, our future...
He found it!!!!

And?!
There's no more poison in Erza-san's body.
I've finished.
Ohh!
eah !!!
Mm...
Wendy!
SST
すっ
Once and only once.
Carla!!
KLAPP
ぱちん
All right!!!
Lucy, high five!!!
WAAAH
ぱちーん
KLAPP
ぱんっ!

Thank you!
KLAPP
But she's out of danger.
I doubt she'll be able to wake up for a while.
Don't ask Wendy to do any more Sky Magic, please.
Now listen.
Is this what Sky Magic can do?
Amazing Her colo is much better no
You're too close!

Now when Erza-san awakens, it is time for our counter attack.
But what I did...
Don't worry about me!
As you can see, this magic uses quite a lot of her magical strength.
Right !!!
Time to take down the Oración Seis!
We'll never let hem have Nirvana !!!!
Yeah !!!!

FASSH
What ?!
That's ...
A pilla of blac light...
It can't be...

オオオ
NIRVANA
!!!!
.....

It's ours !!!!
It belongs to us now!!!!

N-No doubt about it...
Father ...
I'll kill all of the guild members before the middle of the night is on us.
Congratulations.
That light...
You don't think the Oración Seis have beaten us to it, do you?!
Is that Nirvana ...?!
Father, you should go to the light.
Hm...

That's where Jellal is !!!!

JELLAL?!

It's ...
It's ll my ault...
What do you mean, "Jellal" ?!!
ZHOOM
Natsu !!!!
I can't allow them to meet...
...Jellal and Erza !!!!
...to crush im!!!!
I'm going ...

Remarks

An Air Magic wizard working at the Blue Pegasus guild. Air Magic allows one to send waves of air, steal the oxygen out o the air around one's opponent and more It's pretty difficult magic to face.
He placed tanning lacrima in the guild's training gym and sauna, so his perfect tan is due to the guild's support and lacrima crystals.
Tanning Lacrima is a magic item meant to give artificial sun tans. By adjusting the lacrima memory, you can tan to any shade you want in five minutes. The dial can be set to some mysterious number like 61, 63, or 65. Ren's is set to 61 - 61.5.

Chapter 142, Darknes

What is that light?
What's going on here?
ヒョオオオ
HYUUUOOO
Look! Something's flowing from that creepy-looking tree over there.
It looks like it's being sucked into that light!
Then that would mean somebody's already discovered where it is, right?!!
It couldn't be that Nirvana is where that light is, could it?!!

Hibiki!!!
PEEP
Hibiki!! What's going on?! Come in!!!

But is the allie guilds or the Oración Seis...?!!

Got it. Then I'll go head toward that light. Take care.
All right. I will continue my efforts to rescue Wendy-chan!!

Dammit!!!
I think this magic power is jamming our telepathi signals!!

Is it him...?!

Lyon!!! Answer me!!!
Lyon!!!

Somebody's to blame for what happened to Lyon-sama...

Dammit!! What is going on?

What was that...?!
It was... Nirvana!
It only means that the seal was broken just now.
However... I *do* smell the scent of money...
Iwa ha ha!!
But relax.
Its main operation has not activated yet.
Should I fight him...? Should I stop Nirvana ...?
I don't have time to waste battling this guy...
EH HEH HEH...
Still... the reason we came here is to punish the Oración Seis!!

!
Oh!
TRMBL
TRMBL
Oh...
Ohh...
Oh!
!
Money... Money... Now we'l be rich...!
Wh-What?! What is it this time...?!
OHHHHH...
Aaaaa !!!!
Explanations come later. Right now, Natsu is...
Natsu... He said something about Jellal...?
I'm going after Natsu-kun.

Ah...
hh...
Erza's gone!!!
What'll I do ...?
It's all my fault...
Erza... You don't think she could have heard the name Jellal, do you...?
What is with that woman?! Without a word of thanks to Wendy...!!!
It's because I cured Jellal...
...and he went out and found Nirvana... Erza-san... Natsu-san...

DOOM!!
WHOOSH
Just what do you think you're doing?!!!
HSSSS!!
Wait--

DMP
How dare you guys do that to Racer ?!!
There's one!! He's one of Fairy Tail!!!
ZAAAN
DMP
DMP
DMP
DMP
DMP
DMP
Jellal...
You're blocking my way!
Get 'im!!!
Yeaaah !!!
Racer saw to our guild personally, so now we'll show you the power of Harpyia Guild!!!

ZUGAGAGA
OUTTA THE WAY !!!!
DMM
You won't even get close !!!!
I can't let him get anywhere near Erza!
GWAAAAAH!!

TMP
TMP
TMP
Sorry to scare you. She's only unconscious.
Why?! Wait, first... Why are we running?!!
We're going after Natsu-kun and Erza-san. We're heading to where that light is.
SHK
SHK
SHK
SHK
TP
TP
TP
t was all I could do.
Well I don't approve! I know Wendy whines a lot, but that violent action...
Abso-lutely!

!!!
If you want the truth...
...I know what this magic, Nirvana, is.
!!!

That's why Ichiya-san, Ren and Eve don't know. The Master only told me.
Being conscious of it is, in and of itself, dangerous.
But because of the nature of the magic, I couldn't tell anyone.

It's an incredibly frightening magic.

What does that mean

It turns light into darkness.
That is Nirvana!

That's the final stage. The first thing that happens when its seal is broken is it shoots off a black light.
Exactly ike that light there.
It switches them?!!
...into darkness ...
Light...
Initially the black light...
...takes people on the edge of light and darkness and makes them switch sides.
...tumble into darkness.
People of the light with strong negative...
KRIK
KRIK
KRIK
KRIK

It's because emotions like guilt are negative feelings. If I hadn't put her out, she might have fallen into the darkness.
"It's because I cured Jellal..."
"It's all my fault..."
So that's why you made Wendy unconscious...
POI
ZLIPP

You really are an idiot!
What'll we do?! I don't get this!

If that rage was for the sake of someone else, then I couldn't say conclusively that it's a negative feeling.
I can't say...
Wait a second! Wouldn't "rage" be the same? Then Natsu woul be in danger, right?!!

When people start thinking in terms of good and evil, it brings on negative feelings without even intending it.
That's why I couldn't tell anyone about the magic.

...those whose hearts are moved by justice and those by evil will find their personalities reversed.
In other words, when the seal was broken on Nirvana...

Nirvana akes these thoughts nd judges them.
Why does this always happen to me...?!
Who's to blame for putting me through this?
If only he didn't exist...
GRN GRN GRN
WHUP
GWAAAAAH!!
What... are you...
KRIKK KRIKK
Geeh...

I have avenged you, Lyon-sama...
But who is next? One of his cronies? Those of Fairy Tail?
Money ...!!!!
OHHHHHH
Money !!!
Money !!!
Wh- What is going on here...?
Moneeeeey !!!!
!

I mean, who really needs it?

Now... I've also decided to foreswear war.
Eh...?
I've...been desperate to reunite with my brother after we were separated... I thought that if I had money, I could find him.
But... I've just realized what a mistake that is.
What a word that is! Overflowing with sweetness and compassion!
The world is filled with love!!!
Oh, yes!! Love!!!
TWIRL
TWIRL
TWIRL
TWIRL
TWIRL
U... Um...
We shall give them lessons in the wonders of love!!!
Now... we shall go together to stop the plans of my former fellows!!!
HUGG
And as long as there is love in the world, nothing is impossible!!!
GLUG
GLUG
GLUG

GUH...
WHUDD
DOOOM
Wh-What's with this guy...
My magic doesn't hit him...
The hunt has begun.

I'm not a nice guy.
UWAAAHHH!!!
EEE!!
Huh
You're still alive?
But... to look at it the other way, all the people in the dark guilds will turn good, right?
...then all of us are going to turn evil?
So if this Nirvana gets to fu power...
For example, if Nirvana were used on a guild...
What ?!
But the truly frightening part of Nirvana is that some of it can be controlled.
I think that's a possibilit

That can be easily accomplished with Nirvana.
...members of the guild might unscrupulously kill their comrades ...
...or the guild might attack another for no reason.
Unless we stop it quickly...
...all the guilds of ight will be wiped out!
DMP
DMP
DMP
DMP
DMP

Chapter 143, Celestial Spirit Brawl

Remarks

The magic of this recent arrival to the Blue Pegasus guild is powerful enough to turn everything visible into a winter wonderland in an instant. His attacks use "snow rocks" and cause avalanches. Before joining the guild, he interned with the Magic Council's enforcement and investigation squad, the Rune Knights. But when the council was disbanded in disgrace, Eve realized that he needed a new future and decided to enter a guild.

You'd better be preparing your soul for death !!!!
Jellal !!!!
DMP
DMP
DMP
DMP
DMP
Gray ?!!
BLUPP
Hm?
H-Hey!
What happened with that fast guy?
What do you think you're doing here?!!
DM
DM
DM
DM
DM

Wake up, idiot!!
PLASH
Oh, come on!!! I'm in a hurry here!!
Tsk!
SHUSH
SHUSH
SHUSH
ズル ZLMM
ZLMM ズル
SHUSH
SHUSH
SHUSH

Urk...
ふらっ
SLUMP
ZLUMM
We're on a raft?!!
SHUSH
SHUSH
SHUSH
SHUSH
SLUMP
ふら
Y-
ou...
URN...
Your weakness is moving vehicles, right?
You fell for it, Natsu.
SHAKEEN
Die!

VEEEEN
ビィィィ!
!!
VYUUM
As she said, moshi-moshi!
What do you think you're doing, Gray?!!

It's stopped, so pull yourself together !!!
It's... moving... and rocking... and rocking me...
Wh-What's this supposed to mean? That Gray has fallen into darkness...?
FWUM
Lu...cy...
You stay out of this, Lucy!
BOKAN
PACHIKK
mph!
BYUUUUN
Natsu!! I'll save you!!!
Information complete!
Happy can fly and carry people. He is no use in battle.
What did you do to Happy ?!
Male cat!!
KERTHUMP
POGEEEH !!!
GAKEEEN

Huh? Wh-What's that mean?!
BLUUSSH
B-BMP
B-BMP
Lucy through Gray's eyes. A new guild member that's his type, so he finds her attractive.
He's fallen into darkness...
What are you talking about? Gray... Sna out of it...
ばっ
WHOOSH
!
Now that's interesting!!!
Ho?! Celestial Spirits, hm...
But despite her looks, she's a pure and simp Celestial Wizard.
I'm rong...
ZUGYAAAAN

Hibiki through Gray's eyes. Handsome member of Blue Pegasus. No known details.
sk! Not enough info.
Eh? He isn't Gray?!
You're not Gray at all.
Who are you?
BLERB
BLERB
BLERB
BLERB
Gray isn't the type to be swayed by that!
That's right! For him to fall into darkness, he has to be on the edge already with negative feelings.
Just who are you?
I wonder? Your type of man has a weakness for girls, right?
ZIM
ZIM
You're...not too bright, are you? She transformed into you like that. That shouldn't fool anybody.
!!
BOMM
Ah! It's me!!

Kyaaa aaaaaa aaaa !!!
MOSHI-MOSHI-MOSHI-MOSHI-MOSHI-MOSHI!
WHOOSH
ばぁ
Tee hee! ♡
BOYOING
HK
!!
Wow... Amazing.
Celestial Information Complete.
This is no time for puns!
She sure is...
R-Rocking...
Sagittarius if you please.

Eh?
THUNK
GAHH!!
What I did...
N-No, I am not...
Wh-What's with the horse...?!! A traitor...?!!
It couldn't be... She manipulated my Celestial Spirit...
KHH...
SLUMP
Hibiki !!!

I open the Horse-Man Gate!
PEEP
I beg your forgiveness, moshi-moshi...
Sagit-tarius, forced gate closure !!!
POMM
I don't need you to tell me that!!
Carla, take Wendy and run!!! This one's dan-gerous!!!
FLAFF
FLAFF
Kill that flying cat!!
No... Well, I... wouldn't dream...
Ehhhhhh?!!
I answer your call, moshi-moshi--
Eh... Huh?
POMM
SAGIT-TARIUS !!!
You can't. I'm the one who called this Celestial Spirit.
WHOOSH
Forced gate closure !!!

Oh, whatever! Now that they've found Nirvana, this kid's usefulness is over anyway.
!!
SHK
SHK
Urg-urg-urg...
Hurry up and shoot that cat !!!
But...
WHOOM
Hiii, Lucy-chan!
Angel-chan has arrived!
Uwaah !!
BLERB
BLERB
BLERB
SHUUM
That's right!
Piirii!! Piirii!
POMM

They're the spirits of the Twin's Gate, Gemini.

I'm a Celestial Wizard too, you know.

That means I have to do something!!
Or the guild will be in grave danger!!!
Hibiki's out.
And Natsu can't fight either.
I...want your keys.
JANK
Lucy-chan!
Good thing we're right by the water!
That means luck is with me!
Gemini, close!
GASH
Open, Gate of the Water Bearer...
SPASH
SPASH

AQUARIUS!!!!
SPASHAAA
Everybody's going down together !!!!
ZUSHUUUUSH
From the start...?!
That was my plan from the start!!!
GM ゴゴゴゴゴゴ
Get her!!! Get me along with her if you have to!!!!

SCORPIO !!!!
BWOOOH
One of the twelve gold keys ?!!
Eh?
Open, Gate of the Scorpion Palace!
KEEEEN
Yee-haah !!!!
DWOOOM
ay !!!

Scorpio!
PURRRR
ごろにゃん
Huuh ?!!
Yeehah! How've you been, Aquarius?
Oh, ever so lonely! Tee hee!
!!!
Th-That can't be...
My boy-friend! ♡
Yeehah! Nice to meet you, Aquarius' owner!
And there it comes !!!!
Just try saying something out of line in front of Scorpio, got it?! And I'll turn you into a soggy corpse...
Yes, Ma'am!
H-Hold it!!! Aquarius, wait!!!
Say! ♡ How about we do some dinner?
I know this restaurant where we can watch the aurora!
Yeehah! So we can go now, right? Angel?
Be my guest.

BACHIKK
If you don't know the compatibilities between Celestial Spirits, little girl, you'll never beat me, you know!
Kyaa!!
POWANN
Noooo !!!
SLSSH
What'll I do... She just took away my strongest spirit...
BLASSH
ZUBASSH
No... I've got one more!!!
My best Celestial Spirit!!!

Open!!! Gate of the Lion Palace!!!! Loke!!!!
Your prince has arrived!!!
GWOOOON
Nothing could be simpler.
Please!! If we don't defeat her, the guild will...!!!
L-Leo...
!!
Open, gate of the white ram!
Heh
Didn't I just say how important compatibilities are?

TO BE CONTINUED

Afterword

"You look like a criminal in your picture for Volume 16!!" is how everyone around me criticized the picture. So this time, you get my regular face.. or so I thought, but I can't seem to get a good picture! For some reason I seem to be in the habit of scowling whenever a picture is taken. Since what seems like forever, people have said that I've got an evil look in my eyes, and when a picture is being taken, it only seems to get worse. So how does a person come up with a natural-looking smile? It's hard!

On a different subject, here in Volume 17, I did it again. An earth-shaking twist!! Jellal's back...!! Yeah, sorry about that. I just wasn't thinking ahead. (laughs) ..... but when I say things like, "I just wasn't thinking ahead," I get letters from fans telling me that when I say such things, it makes them uneasy. I guess so... I guess any fan would feel uneasy when the author of a work they love is an airheaded idiot. I know I say, "I wasn't thinking ahead," or, "I don't know myself what's coming up in the future," but to be a stickler with words, what I really mean is, **"I haven't quite decided which future to choose."** That would be closer to the reality of the situation. With every new plot twist, it presents a number of different possibilities for the story to run. For example, with Jellal back in the picture, I have come up with three different ways that the big picture can play out. I also have come up with quite a few different ways the story will flow until it gets to those three conclusions. This is how I usually work, imagining a wide variety of possibilities. So please don't worry. I'm busy every day worrying over the best way to create a fun, engaging manga that will meet everybody's expectations. Well... There are still times when my mind is a complete blank, but you know how it is.

Continued from the left-hand page.

: We've explained a mystery! Ding, ding!

: And we have her signature, "ignoring Lucy's question!"

Mira : Time for the next question.

Most of the names of guilds so far have used the names of mythical beasts, but what's the meaning of Oración Seis?

Lucy : If you want a literal translation:
Oración = Prayer
Seis = Six
That's what the words mean.

Mira : So the meaning of the name is, "Six Prayers"?

Lucy : There's no mythical beast name in that guild though, huh?

Mira : Oh? ..... Sure there is!

Like Cobra, for example.

: That isn't the name of a guild! And it isn't a mythical beast either!!!

: We've explained a mystery! Ding, ding!

Lucy : A-And...the final question.

Please tell me who Lucy is in love with.

Mira : I'd like to know myself.

Lucy : There's nobody with that distinction.

: We've explained a mystery! Ding, ding!

: What? There's that little interest?! But, wait! What's that "Ding, ding" thing you do every time?!

Mira : Ah? Whatever are you talking about?

: I can't understand why you'd play dumb about that...

Mira : Eh heh heh! Well for example, even if it's something of a dubious answer, if I say that at the end, it sounds like the mystery's been explained, right?

Lucy : Just some psychological trick?

: We've explained a mystery! Brinnng!

: Suddenly it changes!!!

We are looking for questions about Fairy Tail! Send yours to:

Kodansha Comics
451 Park Ave. South, 7th Floor
New York, NY 10016

EMERGENCY REQUEST! EXPLAIN THE MYSTERIES OF FAIRY TAIL

: We're here in the "Emergency Request! Explain the Mysteries of Fairy Tail!" corner!!

: I've thought this a bunch of times before, but we actually don't explain all that many mysteries here.

Lucy : Don't say that out loud!!

Mira : Here's the first question for this time.

Why is Happy's stomach in Volume 16 blue instead of white?

Vol. 10

Vol. 16

: Th-That's just a mistake, right? And this isn't so much a question as pointing out the mistake.

Mira : There!! We've explained a mystery! Ding, ding!

Lucy : .....

Mira : Continuing on, this is the next question.

Has Elfman now learned to do Satan Soul?

Lucy : I wonder. Well, Mira-san? As his sister, what do you say?

: Not a chance.

: Whoa!! A decisive rejection!

Mira : That isn't what I mean. We each have separate and different magics. Even if they're similar.

Lucy : Eh? Is that right?

Mira : What my sister, Lisanna, used was ***Animal Soul***. A Takeover using the power of animals.

: Really?

Mira : Elfman's is ***Beast Soul***. It's a Takeover using the power of a monster.

Lucy : Uh-huh, uh-huh.

Mira : And mine is ***Satan Soul***, a Takeover using the power of a devil.

Lucy : That certainly makes everybody seem different. But are monsters and devil in different categories?

Continued on the right-hand page.

TAIL de ART

The Fairy Tail Guild de Art is an explosion of fan art! Please send in your art drawn in black pen on large post-card stock!! Those chosen to be published will get a signed mini poster! ♪ Make sure you write your real name and address on the back of your postcard!

Tokyo, Kōchi Toyoda

▼ This is rather cute. It sort of brings a healing feeling.

Saitama Prefecture, Anzu Ame

▼ It's scary, but a kind of cute Gajeel.

Osaka, Nono-chan

▼ The first Aries artwork in a while!! What'll happen to her next volume?

Osaka, Kaho ★

▼ Short-bangs Angel. Give my regards to Gemini.

Nara Prefecture, Shin Yamaguchi

▼ And so quickly after her first appearance is a Carla picture. She's looking annoyed!

Hiroshima Prefecture, Haeshiiv

▼ An awakened Midnight. Just what kind of power does he have?

Niigata Prefecture, Nakanishi

▼ Cobra's so popular! Scary!

Shizuoka Prefecture, Kumi Iketani

▼ His scarf is way too long!

Send to Hiro Mashima, Kodansha Comics
451 Park Ave. South, 7th Floor New York, NY 10016

FAIRY GUILD

illustrations!!

Tokyo, Lio

▼ His face is so big, it's busting out of the card!

Tokyo, Rei6

▼ Sherry with a makeover. I wonder if she'll show up a lot?

Shizuoka Prefecture, Haruka Hirayama

if they're going to fight again.

Okayama Prefecture, Ayaka Ikeda

▼ This one's so cute, I have to put it in here!

Osaka, Mariami Takeda

REJECTION CORNER

Nara Prefecture, Yama-san

▲ Yeah, I didn't mean to, but I laughed. D-Dammit... Ha ha ha...

Any letters and post cards you send means that your personal information such as your name, address, postal code, and other information you include will be handed over, as is, to the author. When you send mail, please keep that in mind.

Translation Notes:

Page 6, All's fair in money and war

Hoteye has an obsession with money, and as such, he tend to confuse classic proverbs by adding the word money in place of the original word. In Japanese, he took the proverb, *Koi ni jouge no hetate-nashi* ("Love doesn't recognize any higher or lower ranks") and changed the word for love, *koi*, to money, *okane*, to make his new proverb. This translation took an English proverb that also involved love (and the general idea) and substituted in "money."

Page 24, Priestess receiving the words of the Gods

In Japanese they were referring to the *miko* of ancient Japan who, unlike their modern counterparts, were the main priestesses of the Shinto religion. The first *miko* recorded is the Empress Himiko of the third-century Japanese country of Yamatai described in a small section of the Chinese epic, Romance of the Three Kingdoms.

Page 119, I'm taking you with me!

What he said in Japanese was a phrase (*ichinin-issatsu* or "One Man, One Kill") that is one of the slogans for the radical, ultra-nationalist right-wing extreme of Japanese politics. The movement espouses some violent ideals such as dying in order to kill someone else *(ichinin-issatsu)*, and killing one for the good of many, *(issatsu-tashô)*. On a lighter note, Japanese baseball has taken this same term of *ichinin-issatsu* to describe a relief pitcher who is called in to face one and only one batter before the next relief pitcher is brought in.

Page 183, There it comes

In Japanese, Lucy used the now-famous Japanese phrase *Kitaaaaa!* to describe the scene with Scorpio. The phrase which literally means "He/She/It is here!" was popularized by the novel-cum-entertainment phenomenon Densha Otoko (Trainman). Although the Trainman fad has come and gone, the phrase still survives. I can't say I'm exactly sure just what Lucy is referring to. It could be the hand gestures which resemble the hand gestures of some good-looking Japanese male pop idols and celebrities. Or it could be the "boyfriend" himself.

Preview of Fairy Tail, volume 18

We're pleased to present you an unlettered preview from Fairy Tail, volume 18. Please check our website (www.kodanshacomics.com) to see when this volume will be available.

ゴゴゴ
ゴゴゴ

がし

ギイイイー
ギンンンンン
ドゴ
ドゴ
ドゴ

ジャリ

カチ
カチ
カチ

ドキッ
ドキッ
ぎゃあああああ
がくん
!

ばしゃ
ハァハァ
ハァハァ
ドッ
ドドドドドド
ズボボボ

ゴッ!!
ハハ…

NEGIMA!™

MAGISTER NEGI MAGI

BY KEN AKAMATSU

Negi Springfield is a ten-year-old wizard teaching English at an all-girls Japanese school. He dreams of becoming a master wizard like his legendary father, the Thousand Master. At first his biggest concern was concealing his magic powers, because if he's ever caught using them publicly, he thinks he'll be turned into an ermine! But in a world that gets stranger every day, it turns out that the strangest people of all are Negi's students! From a librarian with a magic book to a centuries-old vampire, from a robot to a ninja, Negi will risk his own life to protect the girls in his care!

Ages: 16+

Special extras in each volume! Read them all!

VISIT WWW.KODANSHACOMICS.COM TO:

- View release date calendars for upcoming volumes
- Find out the latest about new Kodansha Comics series

Negima © Ken Akamatsu / KODANSHA LTD. All rights reserved.

AIR GEAR

BY OH!GREAT

Itsuki Minami needs no introduction—everybody's heard of the "Babyface" of the Eastside. He's the strongest kid at Higashi Junior High School, easy on the eyes but dangerously tough when he needs to be. Plus, Itsuki lives with the mysterious and sexy Noyamano sisters. Life's never dull, but it becomes downright dangerous when Itsuki leads his school to victory over vindictive Westside punks with gangster connections. Now he stands to lose his school, his friends, and everything he cares about. But in his darkest hour, the Noyamano girls give him an amazing gift, one that just might help him save his school: a pair of Air Trecks. These high-tech skates are more than just supercool. They'll enable Itsuki to execute the wildest, most aggressive moves ever seen—and introduce him to a thrilling and terrifying new world.

Ages: 16+

Special extras in each volume! Read them all!

VISIT WWW.KODANSHACOMICS.COM TO:

- View release date calendars for upcoming volumes
- Find out the latest about new Kodansha Comics series

Air Gear © Oh!great / KODANSHA LTD. All rights reserved.

THEIR MAGIC SPELLS DESTRUCTION!

ARTWORK SUBJECT TO CHANGE

FAIRY TAIL
フェアリーテイル

- PART 2 -

DVD & BLU-RAY COMBO PACK

AVAILABLE NOW!

- PART 3 - AVAILABLE 01.31.2011!

YOU SHOULD BE WATCHING FUNIMATION.COM/FAIRY-TAIL

Kodansha FUNIMATION

Based on the manga "Fairy Tail" by Hiro Mashima, originally serialized in the weekly Shonen Magazine published by KODANSHA LTD. ©Hiro Mashima / KODANSHA/Fairy Tail Guild - TV TOKYO. Licensed by Kodansha Ltd. ©FUNIMATION® Productions, Ltd. All Rights Reserved.

Fairy Tail volume 17 s a work of fiction. Names, characters, places, and incidents are the products of the author's imagination or are used fictitiously. Any resemblance to actual events, locales, or persons, living or dead, is entirely coincidental.

A Kodansha Comics Trade Paperback Original

Fairy Tail volume 17 copyright © 2009 Hiro Mashima
English translation copyright © 2012 Hiro Mashima

All rights reserved.

Published in the United States by Kodansha Comics, an imprint of Kodansha USA Publishing, LLC., New York.

Publication rights for this English edition arranged through Kodansha Ltd., Tokyo.

First published in Japan in 2009 by Kodansha Ltd., Tokyo.

ISBN 978-1-612-62054-1

Printed in the United States of America.

www.kodanshacomics.com

9 8 7 6 5 4 3 2 1

Translator/Adapter: William Flanagan
Lettering: AndWorld Design

TOMARE!

You're going the wrong way!

Manga is a completely different type of reading experience.

To start at the *beginning,* go to the *end!*

at's right! Authentic manga is read the traditional Japanese way—om right to left, exactly the *opposite* of how American books are ad. It's easy to follow: Just go to the other end of the book and read ch page—and each panel—from right side to left side, starting at e top right. Now you're experiencing manga as it was meant to be!